For Rhydian R.L.

First published in North America in 2001 by

LOYOLAPRESS.

3441 N. ASHLAND AVENUE
CHICAGO, ILLINOIS 60657

Original edition published in English
under the title *The Lord is My Shepherd*
by Lion Publishing plc
Sandy Lane West, Oxford, England
www.lion-publishing.co.uk
Copyright © Lion Publishing plc 2001

ISBN 0-8294-1652-8

Typeset in 28/44 Baskerville MT Schoolbook
Printed and bound in Malaysia

00 01 02 03 04 / 10 9 8 7 6 5 4 3 2 1

The Lord Is My Shepherd

Psalm 23

retold and illustrated by

Rob Lewis

LOYOLAPRESS.
CHICAGO

The Lord is my shepherd.

I have everything I need.

He lets me rest in fields
of green grass.

He leads me to quiet pools
of clear water.

He gives me strength
when I am weary.

He shows me the path
I should follow.

If the path I walk goes through
a dark and awful place,
I will not be afraid, for you, Lord,
are with me.

With your shepherd's staff,
you protect me.

You prepare a party for me
as those who want to hurt me look on.

You welcome me to the party
and give me more than I can hold!

I know you will love me
and be good to me
every day of my life.

And I know that your house
will be my home always.

This prayer to God was written long ago by a shepherd boy named David. He knew how to take care of his sheep in the calm and sunny daytime and in the dark and scary nighttime.

When he grew up, David became a rich king. He knew that God took good care of him always, in good times and in bad times.

You can read David's prayer in the Bible in the book of Psalms.